PIANO • VOCAL • GUITAR

TOP CHRIST

2015-2016

ISBN 978-1-4950-5447-1

HAL•LEONARD®
CORPORATION
7777 W. BLUEMOUND RD. P.O. BOX 13819 MILWAUKEE, WI 53213

Visit Hal Leonard Online at
www.halleonard.com

AT THE CROSS
(Love Ran Red)

Words and Music by MATT REDMAN,
JONAS MYRIN, CHRIS TOMLIN,
ED CASH and MATT ARMSTRONG

BECAUSE HE LIVES, AMEN

Words and Music by WILLIAM J. GAITHER,
GLORIA GAITHER, DANIEL CARSON,
CHRIS TOMLIN, ED CASH, MATT MAHER
and JASON INGRAM

* *Recorded a half step higher.*

BEYOND ME

Words and Music by TOBY MCKEEHAN
and DAVID ARTHUR GARCIA

Moderate Pop beat

Call it a rea - son to re - treat; __

I got some dreams that are big - ger than me. __ I might be

out - matched, __ out - sized, __ the un - der - dog __ in the fight of my life.

Recorded a half step lower.

BROTHER

Words and Music by NATHANIEL "BO" RINEHART,
WILLIAM "BEAR" RINEHART and GAVIN DeGRAW

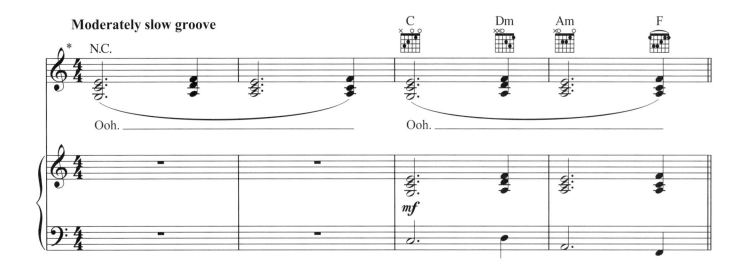

Ooh. _____ Ooh. _____

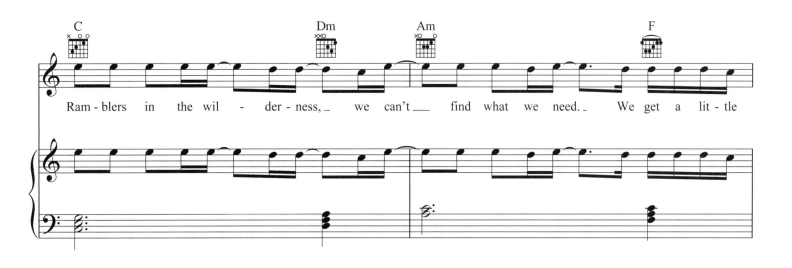

Ram-blers in the wil-der-ness,_ we can't_ find what we need._ We get a lit-tle

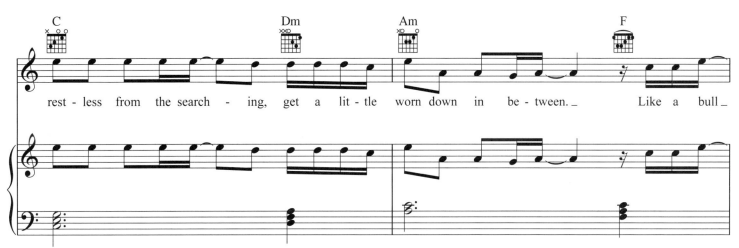

rest-less from the search - ing, get a lit-tle worn down in be-tween._ Like a bull_

Recorded a half step lower.

COME AS YOU ARE

Words and Music by DAVID CROWDER,
MATT MAHER and BEN GLOVER

EVEN SO COME
(Come Lord Jesus)

Words and Music by CHRIS TOMLIN,
JASON INGRAM and JESS CATES

All of cre - a - tion,   all of the earth,   make straight a high - way,   a

Call back the sin - ner,   wake up the saint,   let ev - 'ry na - tion

FIRST

Words and Music by HANK BENTLEY,
MIA FIELDES, JASON INGRAM,
PAUL MABURY and LAUREN DAIGLE

Be-fore I bring my need, I will bring my heart.
Be-fore I speak a word, let me hear Your voice.

Be-fore I lift my cares,
And in the midst of pain,

I will lift my arms.
let me feel Your joy.

FLAWLESS

Words and Music by BART MILLARD,
MIKE SCHEUCHZER, NATHAN COCHRAN,
ROBSHAFFER, BARRY GRAUL, SOLOMON OLDS,
DAVID GARCIA and BEN GLOVER

Moderate Rock beat

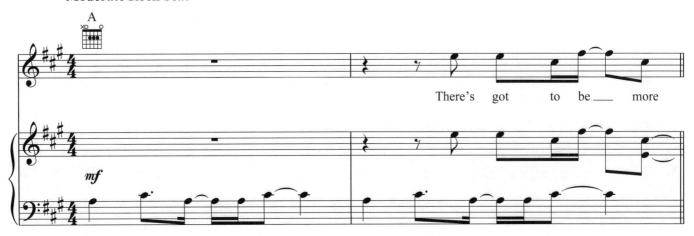

There's got to be ___ more

than go-ing back and forth, from do-ing right ___

___ to do-ing wrong, ___ 'cause we were taught ___ that's who ___ we are. ___ Well, come on,

DROPS IN THE OCEAN

Words and Music by JASON INGRAM,
MATT BRONLEEWE and JON STEINGARD

Moderately fast

I want you as you are, not as you ought-a be.

Won't you lay down your guard and come to Me?

G   A(add4)   Bm7

The shame that grips you ___ now ___ is crip - pl - ing.

G   D   Asus   D/F#

It breaks My heart to ___ see ___ you suf - fer - ing, 'cause I am for ___

Gsus2   Bm7   Asus   A

___ you. I'm not a - gainst ___ you.

Gsus2   D

If you wan - na know how far My love ___ can go, just how deep, ___

f

GOOD GOOD FATHER

Words and Music by PAT BARRETT
and ANTHONY BROWN

it's who You are, _____ and I'm loved _ by You. It's who I am, __

it's who I am, __ it's who I am. _____ You're a good, _____ good Fa-

slight rit.

I AM NOT ALONE

Words and Music by MIA FIELDES, KARI JOBE,
MARTY SAMPSON, BEN DAVIS, GRANT PITTMAN,
DUSTIN SAUDER and AUSTIN DAVIS

Gently, with reflection

When I walk ___ through deep wa - ters,

I know that You will be ___ with me. ___

HOLY SPIRIT

Words and Music by KATIE TORWALT
and BRYAN TORWALT

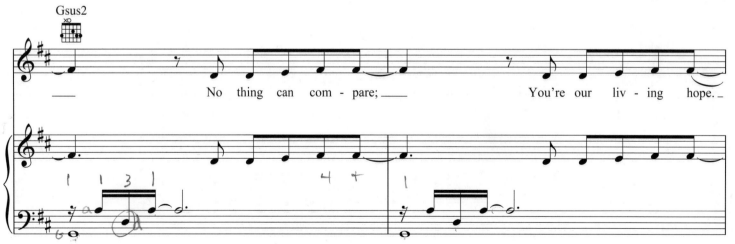

Lyrics:

done. ___ Your pres - ence, ___

___ Lord.

Ho - ly Spir - it, You are wel - come here. Come flood this place and fill the

at - mos - phere. Your glo - ry, God, is what our hearts long for, to be

88

HOW CAN IT BE?

Words and Music by JASON INGRAM,
PAUL MABURY and JEFF JOHNSON

THE RIVER

Words and Music by JOSH SILVERBERG,
COLBY WEDGEWORTH and JORDAN FELIZ

* *Recorded a half step lower.*

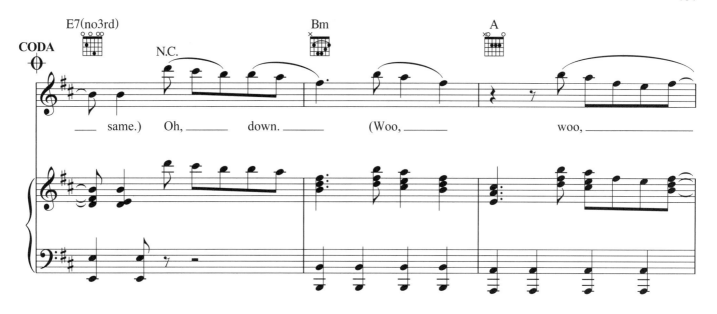

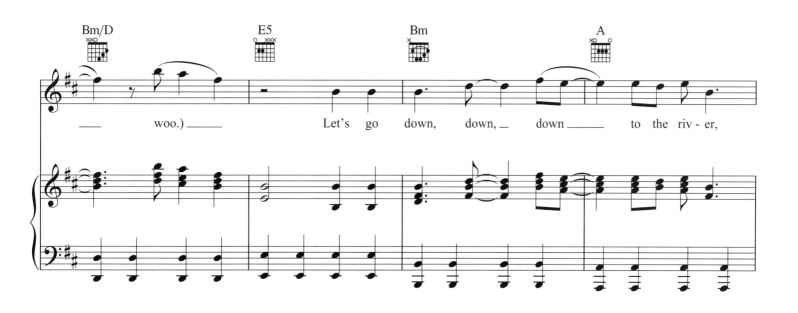

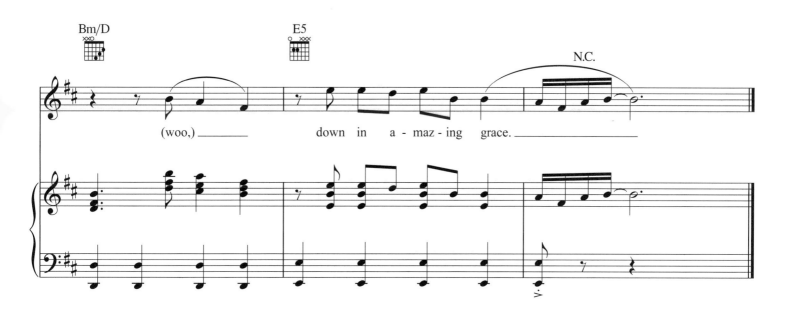

JUST BE HELD

Words and Music by MARK HALL,
MATTHEW WEST and BERNIE HERMS

SAME POWER

Words and Music by JEREMY CAMP
and JASON INGRAM

SOUL ON FIRE

Words and Music by BRENTON BROWN,
MAC POWELL, TAI ANDERSON, MARK LEE,
DAVID CARR and MATT MAHER

Recorded a half step lower.

SHOULDERS
(On Your Shoulders)

Words and Music by BEN GLOVER,
JOEL SMALLBONE, LUKE SMALLBONE
and TEDD TJORNHOM

When con - fu - sion's my com - pan-

THROUGH ALL OF IT

Words and Music by MOLLY E. REED
and BEN GLOVER

TOUCH THE SKY

Words and Music by JOEL HOUSTON,
DYLAN THOMAS and MICHAEL GUY CHISLETT

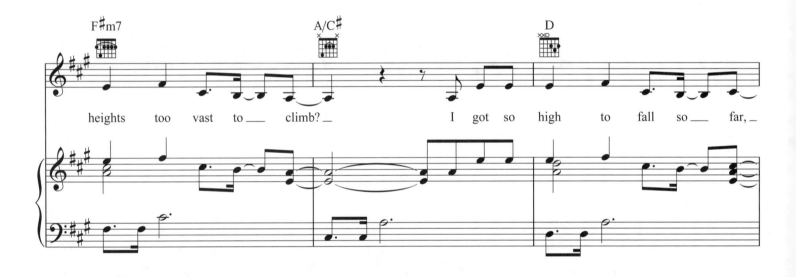

YOU WILL NEVER RUN

Words and Music by
REND COLLECTIVE

Joyfully

You will nev-er run a-way, You're for-ev-er mine.

You will nev-er run a-way, You're by __ my __ side. (Oh. _____

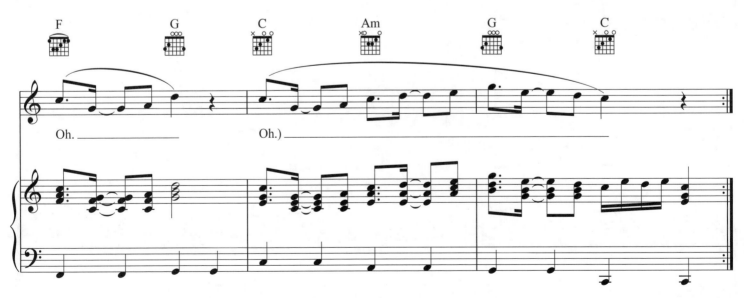

Oh. _____ Oh.) _____

WHO I AM

Words and Music by MIA FIELDES,
SETH MOSLEY and BLANCA REYES

Contemporary Christian Artist Folios from Hal Leonard
Arranged for Piano, Voice and Guitar

CASTING CROWNS – THRIVE
All the tracks from this popular Christian band's 2014 album, including the lead single "All You've Ever Wanted," plus: Broken Together • Dream for You • Follow Me • House of Their Dreams • Just Be Held • Thrive • and more.
00125333 P/V/G.............$16.99

THE JEREMY CAMP COLLECTION
A collection of 21 of this Dove Award-winner's best, including: Empty Me • Healing Hand of God • Jesus Saves • Let It Fade • Right Here • Stay • Take You Back • Walk by Faith • and more.
00307200 P/V/G.............$17.99

DAVID CROWDER*BAND – GIVE US REST
14 songs: After All (Holy) • Because He Lives • Come Find Me • Fall on Your Knees • I Am a Seed • Jesus, Lead Me to Your Healing Waters • Let Me Feel You Shine • Oh, Great Love of God • A Return • Sometimes • and more.
00307390 P/V/G....................$16.99

THE KIRK FRANKLIN COLLECTION
16 of Kirk Franklin's most popular gospel hits: Declaration (This Is It) • Help Me Believe • I Smile • Lean on Me • Looking for You • Jesus • Now Behold the Lamb • Stomp • Whatcha Lookin' 4? • Why We Sing • and more.
00307222 P/V/G.............$17.99

THE VERY BEST OF HILLSONG
25 songs from the popular worldwide church including: Came to My Rescue • From the Inside Out • Hosanna • I Give You My Heart • Lead Me to the Cross • Mighty to Save • Shout to the Lord • The Stand • Worthy Is the Lamb • and more.
00312101 P/V/G.............$17.99

HILLSONG LIVE – GOD IS ABLE
11 songs from the 20th album by musicians and songwriters of Hillsong Church: Alive in Us • Cry of the Broken • The Difference • God Is Able • The Lost Are Found • My Heart Is Overwhelmed • Narrow Road • Rise • Unending Love • With Us • You Are More.
00307308 P/V/G....................$16.99

KARI JOBE – WHERE I FIND YOU
12 songs from Jobe's sophomore CD: Find You on My Knees • Here • Love Came Down • One Desire • Rise • Run to You (I Need You) • Savior's Here • Stars in the Sky • Steady My Heart • We Are • We Exalt Your Name • What Love Is This.
00307381 P/V/G....................$16.99

THE BEST OF MERCYME
20 of the best from these Texan Christian rockers, including: All of Creation • Beautiful • Bring the Rain • God with Us • Here with Me • Homesick • The Hurt and the Healer • I Can Only Imagine • Move • Word of God Speak • and more.
00118899 P/V/G.............$17.99

MERCYME – WELCOME TO THE NEW
This 2014 album reached #1 on the Billboard® Top Christian Album charts and as high as #4 on the Billboard® 200 album charts. Our matching songbook includes all ten tracks from the CD: Burn Baby Burn • Flawless • Greater • New Lease on Life • Shake • Welcome to the New • and more.
00128518 P/V/G....................$16.99

THE BEST OF PASSION
Over 40 worship favorites featuring the talents of David Crowder, Matt Redman, Chris Tomlin, and others. Songs include: Always • Awakening • Blessed Be Your Name • Here for You • How Marvelous • Jesus Paid It All • My Heart Is Yours • Our God • 10,000 Reasons (Bless the Lord) • You Are My King (Amazing Love) • and more.
00101888 P/V/G....................$19.99

PASSION – LET THE FUTURE BEGIN
This matching songbook features the lead single "The Lord Our God," plus: Burning in My Soul • Children of Light • Come to the Water • In Christ Alone • Revelation Song • Shout • We Glorify Your Name • and more.
00119271 P/V/G.............$16.99

PHILLIPS, CRAIG & DEAN – THE ULTIMATE COLLECTION
31 songs spanning the career of this popular CCM trio: Favorite Song of All • Hallelujah (Your Love Is Amazing) • I Want to Be Just Like You • Shine on Us • Your Grace Still Amazes Me • and more.
00306789 P/V/G.............$19.95

MATT REDMAN – SING LIKE NEVER BEFORE: THE ESSENTIAL COLLECTION
Our matching folio features 15 songs, including "10,000 Reasons (Bless the Lord)" and: Better Is One Day • The Father's Song • The Heart of Worship • Love So High • Nothing but the Blood • and more.
00116963 P/V/G....................$16.99

SWITCHFOOT – THE BEST YET
This greatest hits compilation features the newly released song "This Is Home" and 17 other top songs. Includes: Concrete Girl • Dare You to Move • Learning to Breathe • Meant to Live • Only Hope • Stars • and more.
00307030 P/V/G.............$17.99

TENTH AVENUE NORTH – THE LIGHT MEETS THE DARK
The very latest from this Florida CCM band contains 11 songs, the hit single "You Are More" and: All the Pretty Things • Any Other Way • Empty My Hands • Healing Begins • House of Mirrors • Oh My Dear • On and On • Strong Enough to Save • The Truth Is Who You Are.
00307148 P/V/G....................$16.99

THIRD DAY – LEAD US BACK: SONGS OF WORSHIP
All 12 tracks from Third Day's first collection of all-orginal worship songs: Father of Lights • He Is Alive • I Know You Can • In Jesus Name • Lead Us Back • Maker • The One I Love • Our Deliverer • Soul on Fire • Spirit • Victorious • Your Words.
00145263 P/V/G....................$16.99

CHRIS TOMLIN – BURNING LIGHTS
A dozen songs from the 2013 release from this Christian songwriting giant! Includes the lead single "Whom Shall I Fear (God of Angel Armies)" plus: Awake My Soul • Countless Wonders • God's Great Dance Floor • Lay Me Down • Sovereign • and more.
00115644 P/V/G....................$16.99

CHRIS TOMLIN – LOVE RAN RED
Matching piano/vocal/guitar arrangements to Tomlin's 2014 release featuring 12 tracks: Almighty • At the Cross (Love Ran Red) • Fear Not • Greater • Jesus Loves Me • The Roar • Waterfall • and more.
00139166 P/V/G.............$16.99